<u>Dedication</u>

To parents, carers and professionals, you know why!

Andrea Chatten Msc, MBPsS, PGCL&M, Bed(Hons), Dip.CBT

Andrea has been a specialised teacher for over 25 years, working with children from ages 5-16 with emotional and behavioural difficulties. She is currently Director and 'Lead Children's Emotional & Behavioural Psychologist' at Unravel CEBPC Ltd with schools and families in and around Sheffield.

Developing positive, trusting relationships has always been at the heart of her practice with children and young people to nudge them into improved psychological well-being. Over the years, Andrea has developed and applied many positive developmental psychology approaches.

This insight is incorporated into her stories, in order to help children, young people and their families to gain more understanding and potential strategies to try to deal with a range of behavioural issues which children and young people could experience.

Andrea created 'The Blinks' so that parents could also benefit from reading the books with their children, especially if they identify with the children in the stories and their family circumstances. Both parent and child can learn how to manage early forms of psychological distress as a natural part of growing up, rather than it become problematic when not addressed in its early stages.

'The Blinks' is a series of books which discreetly apply lots of psychological theory throughout the stories, including Cognitive Behavioural Therapy, Developmental and Positive Psychology approaches.

This, book 4 in the series, aims to help children understand sadness and the importance of changing some of our behaviours in order to improve positive well-being.

Book 1 in the series tackles the issue of worry and how to prevent this everyday cognition from becoming a more serious anxiety in the future. Book 2 – Anger helps children understand the physiological aspects of anger, what can trigger it and most importantly, how to control it.

Book 3 – Self-esteem subtly educates children and young people on the importance of liking themselves and learning to accept their flaws, so they have more realistic expectations of themselves and their well-being.

Introduction

The Blinks' books have been created to
help children, young people and their
families understand the deeper feelings
that can lead to emotional and behavioural
issues. Combining better understanding of
emotions with the strategies and techniques
provided in this book, we can help children
and young people manage and change the
complexity and duration of difficult feelings
and behaviours over time.

The fourth Blinks' book 'Sad' follows the life of Shan, who experienced sad feelings
internally for many years. This impacted on her sense of self and her motivations for
basic daily functions such as eating, sleeping and exercise. As her on-going sadness
worsens, her resilience, her choices, her relationships and her family are all affected.

Sadness is normal and it is usual to experience this emotion as part of everyday life.
For example, we feel sad when someone dies, or if we don't do very well at something,
or if things change quickly or don't turn out as we would have liked. Sad feelings
are normal reactions to upsetting, unsettling or difficult experiences. However, Shan
experiences sadness quite intensely for a long period of time and it begins to become a
problem.

As with all The Blinks' books, help becomes available and Marlowe Mindful befriends
Shan to help her to understand her sadness and support her to begin to make positive
changes. Our feelings are triggered by events or situations, but we do have the power
to decide how much we pay attention to our feelings and let them take a grip of us. We
each decide how sad, worried or anxious we become. Over time, by changing how we

think and act, we can change what we feel. It is important to remember this crucial formula of understanding our thoughts, feelings and actions, which lay down the foundations towards positive change and improved well-being.

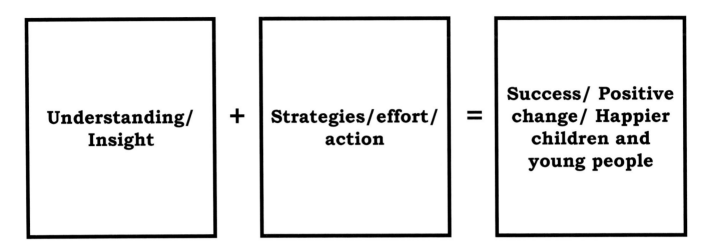

This book aims to help you, as the supportive adult in a child or young person's life, to understand the psychological theory behind The Blinks' interventions, which were used to support Shan with her sadness. The more empowered we are about our understanding of difficult feelings, the more confident we can be to guide and nudge the children and young people in your care towards improved understanding and emotional freedom, rather than resistance.

Section 1 - The Psychology of Sadness.

Sadness is a normal emotion, most often triggered by feelings of difficulty, helplessness, loss or pain. When we feel sad, we often become quiet, less energetic and withdrawn. This can reduce us from our greater and better self, to a smaller presence.

In fact, sadness can be bittersweet.

Although it is a normal response to an emotional wound that will heal over time, the way we experience sadness is as unique to us as our fingerprint. Just as adults do, children face difficult realities and experience emotional pain, for example from rejection, frustration, a sense of failure, illness or death. These incidents can become sad memories that are banked in our memory if we can't make sense of them, particularly at a young age. Sometimes such early life experiences, if never verbalised or understood, can have a long term effect or be carried with us throughout our lifetime. It is therefore important for children and young people to understand this emotion and learn to see it has both positives and value.

Sadness can make us feel awakened. It can help us value the good we may have lost. It can make us feel humble and kind. It can allow us to feel greater empathy and compassion for those who have gone through or are going through similar experiences. It can also remind of the importance of the support we may have received from other people and motivate us to offering support in return; such give and take is an important part of our human experience. We all need to receive love, but it is also important for well-being to give love.

Sadness can help us fully evaluate and appreciate our happier times.This fosters the feeling of awe, which is thought to be the most joyful and invigorating feeling we can reach. In order to feel true awe, it is estimated that around one third of our experiences need to be difficult or generate sadness. It is only through this emotional off-setting, that we are able to feel the wonder, magic and value of the many good times and good things in our lives.

Like all other emotions, sadness is an important tool in helping us to understand what is going on inside us and around us. Sadness should not be seen as a negative emotion that we must not allow ourselves to feel. Sadness can have many positive side effects which facilitates a better recovery over time, such as closer connections with others, greater empathy and understanding of a situation, increased compassion from others (Shan's teacher, Mr Pryce, being a prime example), an understanding of what to to do to avoid danger or harm from sadness in the future or even a meaningful flash of joy that reminds us we are worth more than how the sadness is making us feel and helps us value our lives more.

As with many emotional states, sadness is a temporary change of feelings that lowers our mood and we often cry as a result of feeling sad. We must remember that sadness is an everyday emotion which can come and go and can range in its intensity from mild to severe.

Sadness can often be mistakenly confused with depression (link is external). Depression can appear with no obvious triggering event and can result from an unhealthy, maladaptive reaction to a painful experience, which we try to ignore, resist from dealing with or become overwhelmed by. When we're in a state of depression, our positive emotions can often feel numb or even dead. Negative feelings of shame, self-blame or self-loathing begin to become more dominant and can have a huge impact on our choices, behaviours, energy levels and well-being. Sadness, however, can provide an awakening.

Shan's severe sadness could possibly be signs of early depression as hers is a persistent and intense lowered mood, as well as beginning to disrupt her ability to function in day to day tasks. However, the earlier that positive action starts, the quicker these difficult feelings begin to ease, developing and reinforcing the importance of emotional intelligence.

Most of us would do our best to avoid feeling sad if we could, but this isn't always the best option. Suppressing unpleasant feelings because we're fearful of how difficult we might find them, can only make us feel worse at some point in the future. This could be partly due to:

- not reflecting on the issues that have led to the sadness in the first place and therefore not learning from it or making any changes;
- not making the best life decisions in order to avoid the reality of dealing with difficult feelings, for example use of drugs or alcohol;
- buried feelings which build up over time - as more difficult feelings are added to what we've buried, this could eventually lead to an emotional breakdown.

We can see how the long term cost of blocking out sadness can be much more severe than allowing ourselves to feel it, deal with it and let it end on its own. The strategies provided in this Blink's novel supports the gentle nudging of the experience of sadness to a healthier level. Emotional resistance to the feelings of sadness can actually have the opposite effect. If we want emotional freedom from difficult emotions, we need to accept them. This mentality is thought to be the healthiest with regard to emotional well-being.

Sadness can actually ground us when we learn to recognise it and let ourselves feel it in a healthy and safe way. This fosters our internal resilience, an important aspect of emotional development. Ignoring and suppressing emotions can actually make us struggle more and may lead to more severe conditions such as depression.

Long term research suggests that when we say we are angry or filled with hate, that we are actually deeply sad or disappointed about something. These hidden emotions are actually driving our angry and hateful feelings and become the ways that we learn to express sadness or disappointment. Understandably, this can lead to further problems over time.

Persistent low mood, as Shan experienced, can be more problematic and can affect our self-esteem and behaviours, as well as activating physiological symptoms that could be misdiagnosed as physical illness. Shan's resistance to her sadness fuelled her inability to face the day ahead, which lead to her feeling and becoming physically sick. This physical display validated her sadness and anxieties to herself and her family, but also nudged her further away from the demands of everyday life, spending weeks in bed, hiding away.

As with all emotions, this is why it is crucial that we help children and young people to name and claim what they are feeling. The brain activates different emotions as a form a communication to help us process the world around us. Interestingly, if we don't acknowledge our feelings, and instead try to surpress or ignore them, then the brain can turn the volume up on that feeling until we stop long enough to register what we are feeling. When we do this, the brain sighs with relief that we have acknowledged what we are feeeling, allowing us to understand what we are feeling so we can begin to do something about it.

Other words used to describe emotions linked to sadness are:

- depressed
- deflated
- dejected
- despair
- dreary
- disappointed
- distraught
- distressed
- down

- grief

- gloomy

- hurt

- loss

- low

- lonely

- miserable

- regretful

- sorrowful

- unhappy

- upset

Top tips for supporting sadness and low mood:

✓ Help children to name and claim the feeling

✓ Let children know that sadness is okay and can actually be helpful

✓ Remind children that the sadness will go away and that it is a temporary state during difficult times

✓ When a sad mood lingers, help children reduce the time they invest in revisiting sad memories by doing things that they like

✓ Teach children to see the things in their life that they are grateful for. Being grateful about things registers in the reward and pleasure zone of the brain and releases happier chemicals, the same as the effect of anti-depressants. Saying thank you is an action, being grateful is a state of mind

✓ Break the cycle of negativity and low motivation. Eat healthily, exercise, and think more positive thoughts. This will weaken and challenge the low mood cycle

✓ Hug your children as much as possible. This helps children feel connected and it also releases lots more happy hormones

✓ Practise mindful breathing (inhale deeply, then exhale completely for 5 cycles, 4/7/8 breathing (breath in deeply for 4 seconds, hold for 7 seconds, breathe out slowly for 8 seconds). Alternatively, try 3/3/3 (same principles as 4/7/8 but helpful for younger children and for relaxation)

✓ Allow your children to get enough sleep (children up to 8 years – 11/12 hours, up to 13 years – 10/11 hours, 13+ years – 9- 12 hours)

Activities and questions for discussion with children and young people

1. What was the last thing that made you sad?

2. How do you feel when you are sad? I feel...

3. Have you ever felt like Shan?

4. Keep a gratitude log. Write in at least 5 things a day that you are grateful for.

5. Become more mindful. Next time you are walking to school notice:

   ✓ how the ground feels as you walk

   ✓ how your body feels as you move

   ✓ how your clothes feel

   ✓ what the weather feels like on your skin

6. Practise mindful eating. Next time you eat, really eat! How does the food look and smell? What does it sound like in your mouth? How does it feel when you swallow it? What does it taste like? This helps you notice your alive thoughts rather than being ruled by sad memories.

Section 2 – Cognitive Behavioural Therapy (CBT) approaches to support sadness

CBT is a psychology model that helps us understand how our thoughts affect how we feel. This concept fundamentally drives what we believe about ourselves and our world. The principles of CBT are based on two main elements:

1. If we think something for long enough, we will eventually feel it.
2. The longer we feel something, the more likely we are to believe it.

Shan's thoughts are dominated by sad memories which activate sad thoughts and feelings. When Marlowe Mindful begins working with Shan, her sadness could be regarded as severe and problematic. Shan became caught up in many negative thinking patterns which affected her choices and behaviours. Luckily, with the help of Marlowe Mindful, Shan begins to learn about the emotions involved in sadness, and some very important tools to reduce its intensity.

The brain and how we need to help it break negative cycles

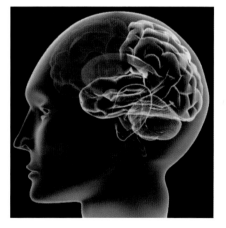

Our brain's main job is to keep help us survive and keep us alive. Yet our brain isn't always our friend! We have automatic responses to what our brain is doing; these processes can sometimes send us off in unhelpful directions. The diagram below shows how our brain functioning can develop some negative self-beliefs:

Thoughts	Feelings	Beliefs
I think no-one likes me	I feel no-one likes me	No-one likes me
I think I am stupid	I feel I am stupid	I am stupid
I think my life is pointless	I feel my life is pointless	My life is pointless

We must try to remember the importance of challenging our thoughts and pass this wisdom on to our children. It is also essential for us to share the knowledge that our brain most often functions on automatic pilot and we need to remember that it is sometimes necessary to activate our 'Master' brain thinking, just like Shan in the story.

In all The Blinks' novels, strategies are taught so that the children in them can learn to develop higher level thinking strategies which can trip out some of the negative spirals that have developed. This is an important aspect of the development of emotional intelligence.

To break low mood, it is crucial to weaken the cycle of thoughts and feelings, but we can only do that if we know what to do and why.

Sadness can be triggered by a difficult life event which has become stored as a sad memory. If we keep revisiting that sad event, then our brain can make other changes which over time, can affect our choices and behaviours, feeding ithe sad mood even further.

Fig 1 – Sadness spiral

From the above diagram (fig 1), we can see how persistent sadness is created by lots of different circuits in the brain malfunctioning. This isn't because the brain *isn't* working properly, it is because it *is*! We can see how different circuits negatively affect others and so drive the intensity and duration of the sadness further. We can then begin to understand how important it is to identify how to break the sadness cycle as well as understand why we are doing what we are doing.

Marlowe Mindful suggested to Shan to reduce the time spent revisiting her sad memories. By doing this, Shan began to make changes one of the malfunctioning circuits as shown in the diagram below (fig 2). By exercising and adopting healthier eating also recommended by Marlowe Mindful, Shan began to change the functioning of two more circuits which not only helped her to feel better, but also weakened the sadness intensity further.

It is important to note that research suggests it takes roughly 28 days to break a cycle of behaviour. Within that time, a person can experience periods of frustration, weakness and even possible relapse in behaviours. The important thing is to keep trying until you are carrying out the desired behaviour subconsciously. These *whys* behind the *whats* can be hugely motivational in helping us to engage fully in the change process and becoming the Master to our automatic functioning.

Fig 2 – Happier Spiral

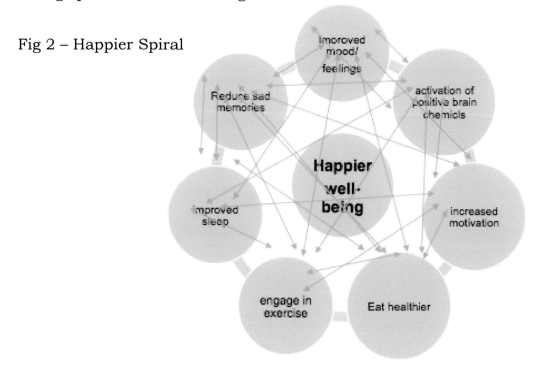

Changing negative self-talk

We can all be guilty of engaging in negative thinking about ourselves. For many of us it can be a default setting which we recognise, but which now motivates us to challenge it and work harder to prove it wrong. Children's and young people's brains are not always developed or skilled enough to recognise this dialogue and do something constructive with it.

As the active adult in the lives of the children in our care, we can sometimes feel a need to try and change this mindset as quickly as possible by offering positive words of reassurance that might help them to recognise that their negative thinking isn't helpful to their well-being.

The two exercises below help identify whether our negative thinking is valid or more extreme than it needs to be. These exercises also allow us to begin the process of reflection and challenge our thoughts with evidence, which are the crucial stages in moving negative thinking forward.

<u>All or nothing - Exercise</u>

Think:

When? Why? How? Who else? Really? Why? Choices? New way? Feedback?

What is the issue?	Reality	Both sides of the issue	What can I choose to do now

<u>Overcoming negative mental moaning - Exercise</u>

Moan!	Response from a friend to the full-on moan!	How is it really?	What's their response to the normal moan	How reasonable from 1-10 is the moan really?

If we feel that the negativity from our children's thinking doesn't seem to be diluting (remember breaking cycles takes time!), it is important to remind yourself that this negative thinking could actually represent more complex feelings. This is destructive dialogue which could have already affected, or begin to negatively affect, who they believe they are. It might also highlight some difficult life event that may be causing them to struggle.

As with all difficult life experiences our children may face, it is important that we are emotionally available to them at the time. Through this compassionate approach, we can be the best support possible in preventing some of these negative thinking patterns becoming negative beliefs. Here's what you can do:

- ✓ Offer empathy and try to understand this in relation to their age and their life
- ✓ Investigate further. Is this just a moan about today or does it show a deeper concern or worry?
- ✓ Challenge the thoughts with evidence (why they are loveable, a good friend, clever etc.)
- ✓ Help them to be kind to themselves. What would they say to their best friend if they were in this position? Help them learn to say this to themselves
- ✓ Focus on solutions. Show them you are a team and that between you, you can find solutions for most things. Feeling your love and support at the time is solution number 1!

ACT (*A*ccept - *C*hoose direction - *T*ake action)

Many of the children, young people and families that I work with struggle with very difficult feelings which impact on their ability to function in day to day life. Sometimes, however, their resistance to the issue and desperation to get rid of their difficult feelings becomes the main issue, burying the other feelings underneath.

Acceptance is a fundamental element in positive well-being and mental health for many reasons. First, it removes the fight we feel towards the issue or the feeling we don't want to have. By accepting the reality of what we are experiencing, we remove the avoidance barriers that were stopping us facing it head on.

Second, it allows for emotional freedom. I once worked with a young girl who was crippled with anxiety. It stopped her being able to go into her lessons, her body was so flooded with anxiety and apprehension that all she could do was shake and cry. One particular day when her anxiety was dominating her, I asked her if she trusted me to try something new. She nodded weakly but I told her that together we were going to invite her anxiety to give it its best. She started shaking her head, unable to even consider this option. After some reassurance using acceptance theory, she was willing to try anything that might improve the prison of her anxiety.

Together we invited her anxiety to give its biggest dose. I held her hand and supported her through what was a really big ask. She did it. The result surprised us both. Her anxiety had gone! By totally and utterly acknowledging its presence and accepting it, the anxiety was released and for the first time, she felt emotional freedom.

This wasn't a miracle and it wasn't the end of her anxiety, but what we had done together that day was change the power balance and start the recovery. This young girl proved she was stronger than she realised. So, point number three is that we don't know what we are capable of until we accept it and try it. Below is a simple ACT exercise for you to try yourself or with your children:

Accept – What is the issue you are struggling with? Be honest! (Remember resistance hasn't worked, so try acceptance.)

Choose direction

- Where do you want to be in a year's time? (think feelings, lifestyle)
- What are the life costs to you living with these intense feelings?
- What are the life benefits to you living with these intense feelings?
- What values/qualities do you hold? (these are personal strengths and traits that will get you where you want to be and last forever).

Take action

✓ What are you going to do to get to your desired direction? (create an action plan, that involves emotional acceptance and regulation, not avoidance and desperation.)

Forever target: What will you do this week to feel like your life is of greater purpose and fulfilment?

Mindfulness

Over the last few years, the concept and value of mindfulness has started to gain real momentum. It is an approach we can all do so easily throughout the day to keep us focused and grounded in our awareness and our bodies.

The act of mindfulness can be incredibly helpful to us in changing the way we think and feel about what we are doing, especially during stressful times, to support us in making wise choices.

Throughout the novel, Marlowe Mindful (aptly named!) helps Shan get in tune with what she is thinking and feeling. Shan also learns how to bring her negative thinking into the present rather than her focus always being in the past, where her sad memories reside.

Many of us, and children even more so, can be dominated by negative pre-occupied thinking styles which prevent us from accessing the wonderfulness that is around us and that we can miss every day. Without building up a catalogue of things that have made us feel good, or have put a smile on our face, we could all too easily become blind to what is right there in front of us.

Mindfulness anchors us into the present moment so that we experience the here and now. More so, it gives us a break from the overthinking part of the brain (the pre-frontal cortex). It is this change in brainwave, even just temporarily, that can contribute to the many benefits mindfulness offers.

By helping children develop mindfulness practice, they too can become fluent in the language of calmness and well-being, and use it as a natural tool to reset their day. Some mindful strategies are:

Mindful breathing – practise focusing on how the breath feels as it comes in and out of their body. Encourage them to hold on to their chest or tummy as they are doing it to anchor themselves in the breathing process. As they become more comfortable, remind them to let any thoughts and feelings go. This time is just for breathing.

5-4-3-2-1 Game – Begin with breathing in deeply and exhaling slowly, then ask children to shut their eyes and imagine:

- ✓ 5 things they can see
- ✓ 4 things they can hear
- ✓ 3 things they can feel
- ✓ 2 things they can smell
- ✓ 1 thing they can taste.

Repeat if necessary.

Mindful eating – As with all mindful activities breathing begins the process. Ask children to select a piece of fruit, or healthy snack. Tell them they are not just going to eat it, they are going to really eat it! Ask them to focus on how the food smells, looks and sounds when they bite it, how it feels in their mouth and what it tastes like. Ask them to chew it as slowly as they can and think about what is happening inside their mouth. Have a breathing break and then continue.

Smell the roses – this age old saying was ahead of its time or is it us who are behind?! This helps children notice their environment and see the beauty in what is around them. Help them think about how the ground feels as they walk on it, and how their body feels as they are walking. Remind them to keep focusing on their breathing throughout.

Top tips to reduce the impact of negative self-talk patterns

- Look at the cost and benefits to problematic situations to motivate you or your child into doing things differently
- Help your children make choices to prove to yourself that you can make positive decisions (remember our brain doesn't need the best choice, just one that is good enough)
- Celebrate mistakes – they are okay. They mean we are learning. Try to use the terminology right and wrong rather than good or bad
- Congratulate the process more than the result. Be impressed by working hard, sticking at difficult tasks, and making right choices
- See the good and remind your children of it often. If they hear positive dialogue from you they will start to embed it
- Empathise- try to put yourself in their shoes so that you have a better understanding as to what they might be feeling. Make statements rather than asking questions, for example, "You look sad" rather than, "Are you ok today? If you are struggling to know what to say, simply ask if they need a hug, or remind them you are always there if they need to talk
- Explore – look deeper into the issue to find out what is really upsetting them. Is it just the maths work they had to do today, or is it all maths?
- Work as a team – not all problems can be solved quickly. Help your children understand that by working together as a team, you can pretty much sort most things. Remind them that sometimes the solution is more abstract, like not giving up or to keep practising
- Change what you/they say – remind children and young people that what we say to ourselves affects what we feel. Instead of "I am so stupid, I always get things wrong." Say "mistakes are normal, they mean I am learning".

- Help children to become their own best friend (compassionate mind theory)

- Challenge thoughts – thoughts are just guesses and not all feelings are facts. Remind your child of difficulties they have faced before and to use evidence to challenge difficult thoughts and feelings

- See the importance of accepting

- Practise mindful breathing with your children whenever possible to reset yourself throughout the day

Questions for discussion with children and young people

1. Do you ever feel like your sad thoughts take over?

2. What do you do when this happens? Are there any other things that might help?

3. What do you think acceptance is? Why could it be important in some situations?

4. Think of something that is on your mind at the moment. Complete this table:

All or nothing - Exercise

Think:

When? Why? How? Who else? Really? Why? Choices? New way? Feedback?

What is the issue?	What is the reality?	What are both sides of the issue	What can I choose to do now

5. Think about a mental moan you have. Complete this table to learn more about it and what to do.

Overcoming negative mental moaning - Exercise

Moan!	Response from a friend to the full on moan!	How is it really?	Their response to the normal moan	How reasonable from 1-10 is the moan really?

Section 3- How sadness affects behaviour and self-esteem, sleep quality and well-being

When we feel sad, it impacts on our behaviours in many ways. Usually the first sign is crying and in itself, this can be a positive way of moving things on. Tears release chemicals that make us feel better. Greater problems can arise if the sadness is hanging around longer than we want it to and by us not knowing what to do with it or change it for the better.

Psychologically, sadness means we are feeling more negative about ourselves and the world around us, and are therefore more likely to notice other things that reinforce our sadness. It can also begin to impact upon our self-confidence and self-esteem by reducing what we feel we are capable of. This process can then begin to activate feelings of anxiety linked to an awareness that what we are feeling isn't changing as quickly as we want it to and a fear that we may never feel happy again which is what was beginning to happen to Shan.

Prolonged sadness can affect our motivations and generally make everyday things seem harder and more challenging. This frustration to our sadness can also be the driver to more angry behaviours, because our tolerance and patience seem to be tested much more when we feel in low mood.

Intense, prolonged sadness can also start affecting our physical health. The t-cell count in our blood needs to be high in order to fight infections and illnesses. However if our mood is low, our t-cell count also starts falling which means that we are more likely to become ill when feeling prolonged sadness. This is never more important than when fighting more serious illnesses, such as cancer. The biggest challenge we have is not letting the thought of cancer weaken our mood too significantly so that we keep out t-cell count up to fight it on our behalf.

Quality of sleep can also change if we are feeling sadder than normal. In fact, poor sleep can sometimes be the pre-cursor to feeling sad as when we are not rested, our brain function and chemical release are also negatively affected. We can see then how sleep problems on top of low mood could then make things worse.

Sleep hygiene, or sleep architecture as it is sometimes known, provides us with evidence that what we do before sleep dictates whether or not our sleep is of a decent quality. Key factors that can support positive sleep are:

- ✓ Try to go to bed at roughly the same time each night and get up roughly the same time each morning
- ✓ Count your sleep in 90 minute cycles. We feel better if we have competed 5 x 90 minute cycles rather than 6.5 x 90 minute cycles. Children need 7-8 cycles, teenagers 6-7 cycles, adults 4-5 cycles
- ✓ Come off all screens at least 60 minutes before sleep as blue light is a stimulant to the brain and so needs time to unwind from it
- ✓ Avoid caffeine and large meals at least 3 hours before bed
- ✓ Have a night time routine to transition from the busy day. Warm bath, hot milk, reading, cleansing routine all help your brain associate with getting ready for sleep
- ✓ Turn down the lights as the sun goes down so that brain knows that night time is approaching and is more likely to release melatonin, ready for sleep time. Turn off any LED lights in your room as the brain can sense these too.
- ✓ Make sure your bedroom is the right temperature and comfortable to sleep in. The brain really doesn't like it if is too messy!

- ✓ Write down any worries before you go to sleep as the brain can't sleep if it is thinking or planning
- ✓ Get comfortable. If you're not comfortable in bed, the brain releases the stress hormone and this impacts on our ability to sleep
- ✓ Breathe. Stop wriggling, lay still and breathe deeply inwards and slowly outwards

Social withdrawal can also be a normal response to feeling sad. In the story Shan didn't feel like she had positive relationships with anyone which led to her withdrawing from those around her. This could initially be because she did not want others to see how she was really feeling, or because she didn't want her loved ones to become concerned about her. Sometimes for all of us, it can be because we need to process what we are feeling sad about before we feel capable of being able to talk about it.

Unfortunately, over time, social avoidance can impact further on sadness by disconnecting us with the love that we desperately need during difficult emotional times. The longer this goes on, the more likely we are to hit a negative spiral as additional loneliness reinforces our sadness further.

As stated in the introductory section, sadness most often activates compassion from our loved ones which strengthens emotional connections, which is what we most desperately need. When our children and young people are sad, it is hugely important to show emotional connection as much as possible.

Hugs, kisses and cuddles communicate love and support. Regular verbal interaction assists them in eventually releasing their sadness. Knowing you are there for them provides evidence that they are not alone.

As parents, carers and professionals, we are always walking the fine line of knowing what we feel is best for the children in our care. Many parents say to me that their kids reject them all the time and put barriers up to them getting close. Sometimes this might be what kids want, but we need to decide whether it is right. Parenting must only ever go one way, from the parent to the child. If we start wavering in doing what we believe our children need because we are fearful they might not like us because of it, we are moving into dangerous territory.

Children and young people test us all the time. Testing us to see how much power they have. Testing to see how quickly we will give in. Testing how strong we are and how much we really care. It is when our children are in their most difficult emotional states that we need to show them the most love and patience. When our children are sad, regardless of how much they are wanting to hide away, prove to them that you are there with warmth and love.

This approach also supports positive self-esteem rather than eroding it. Children and young people are aware how their sadness can change how other people view them so it makes sense that it can certainly have an effect on how they view themselves. By offering unconditional positive regard (an environment of complete acceptance) and supportive reassurance with honest and accurate information, we can prevent another layer of low self-worth being added to the complex pie of emotional difficulties.

It is also a good time here to talk about the value of non-judgmental listening. When we are feeling emotionally vulnerable, it can become very difficult to talk about things, especially if we think we are being a nuisance, or don't feel we deserve to be helped and supported. This can be a huge test for us personally as we all have breaking point. However, if we can dig deep and keep offering love and support during difficult times, the outcome for the future will only ever be better. On difficult days, try and remember that the alternative, *your* emotional withdrawal, is only ever going to make the child or young person feel sadder, alone and rejected, embedding the problem further. Although emotional difficulties are complex, part of the medicine lies within

The Beatles' famous lyrics – "Love is all you need".

<u>*Questions & tasks for discussion with children and young people.*</u>

1. Draw your sadness. What does it look like?

2. What was the last thing that made you sad?

3. How did your sadness make you feel?

4. What did you do when you were sad? (think about changes in your behaviours)

5. When you felt sad, would you have liked from those who love you?

6. How did you move on from your sadness?

Section 4 – Your role in supporting children who feel prolonged sadness and low mood

I spent all of my teaching career working with children who presented with varying degrees of emotional and behavioural difficulties. I have learned more from these children than I have learned from reading. Before I had children of my own, I wasn't sure I was as aware of the enormity that becoming a parent brings.

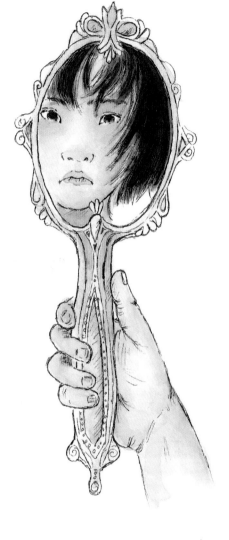

I also believe that the psychology of parenting is very under-rated, as we are steered more towards the act of giving birth rather than what the impact of becoming a parent will have on as human beings, and our own psychological well-being (cue another book!).

When I had my first child, I couldn't wait to take her into school to show her off to the children, parents and teachers. I remember one parent asking me how I was finding parenting. My response was that it was so difficult, much more difficult than I thought it would be. She was shocked at my answer. How could a teacher, who teaches classes of 30+ kids with behavioural difficulties, find looking after one baby harder? I went onto explain that it was because it was so important to me and that made it more difficult because I wanted to do it well and right.

However well we want to parent, as we are all aware, we don't get a reference manual (until now!). The whole purpose of this book is for you to be one step ahead and more of an expert in your child's emotional well-being, as you can then be the best support you can in your most important role as a parent or carer.

This section is aimed at sharing with you some of the most valuable pieces of information that can only help and support you to do what you are doing even better. Those of you that have bought this book have already passed one of the biggest tests in positive parenting, you are reflective. You recognise when things aren't right and you want to do something about it. Well done.

This book in itself, alongside reflective approaches, will not in any way prevent us from making mistakes. As human beings, parents are not perfect, and mistakes can happen. Importantly however, we often don't make the *same* mistakes, and continue to parent with more confidence. This reinforces us as the stable base our children desperately need us to be. So here we go.

Child brain vs adult brain

As we know, children's brains don't begin the process of hardwiring until just before puberty and the process lasts until around the age of 25. During this time, children don't think, feel, reason, question or pre-empt situations in the same way as adults.

Until the age of roughly 8 years old, the child brain only thinks concrete thoughts. For example, if a pet dies before this age, although children may be sad, they don't really understand the true context of death (an abstract thought). Developmentally, they cannot understand the complexity or reality of abstract concepts such as death, and so appear to be not as bothered. When children move into the next developmental stage of abstract thinking, they can better understand things within their context, and so are more likely to respond with deeper emotions.

It is important for us to know this, as many parents worry that their child doesn't present with much compassion or sensitivity in some situations. By recognising that this can be due to their stage of development and not cold heartedness, parental anxiety eases and positive parenting can resume. It would be a good place to reiterate here that as parents, we are a mirror to our children's well-being and vice versa. If our children aren't happy then we aren't happy. If we are anxious and stressed, our children pick up on our heightened emotional state and begin to mirror it. Their behaviour can become more challenging or clingy when we least need it. I call this phase BOPS (Bottom of the Pile Syndrome) and it is most often the symptom of not looking after everyone else's needs before looking after our own well-being.

If ever I have BOPS, everything gets worse. The children play up, things are more likely to go wrong, and generally life feels more emotional and more difficult. As my wise mum always says "If we aren't right, nothing is right," and how right she is. By reflecting, so that we recognise and accept our needs rather than resist them, we can be kinder to ourselves and in turn be better parents, which I find always turns things around.

The important thing to remember here is that children's brains are not adult brains and so they don't feel things in the same way as we might expect them too. It is also important for us adults not to transfer on to them how we think we would feel in a particular situation. We ned to try and check in with our own emotional state as often as possible as, with some hard work and re-tuning, we can reset our brains. Children can only reset theirs with adult guidance and modelling.

Parenting approaches

Positive parenting needs to include lots of loving warmth, support and nurture, as well as an element of 'tough love' which ensures that children develop acceptable expectations and social conduct. There are thought to be four different parenting styles as shown in the table overleaf:

	Supportive Parent is accepting and child-centered	Unsupportive Parent is rejecting and parent-centered
Demanding Parent expects much of child	**Authoritative Parenting** Relationship is reciprocal, responsive; high in bidirectional communication	**Authoritarian Parenting** Relationship is controlling, power-assertive; high in unidirectional communication
Undemanding Parent expects little of child	**Permissive Parenting** Relationship is indulgent; low in control attempts	**Rejecting-Neglecting Parenting** Relationship is rejecting or neglecting; uninvolved

As you can see, when a child receives the balance of support and realistic expectations from a parenting adult, the relationship works well together through honest and open communication, but with firm boundaries in place in order to tweak negative behaviours as not allow bad habits to set in. This Authoritative model is thought to be the most beneficial style of parenting for all children, but more so for children with emotional difficulties. Shan definitely benefitted from this approach as it made her feel like she was more emotionally connected to her parts and they were working together better.

It is very easy to see from the table how an imbalance in the level of support and demand can lead to complications in relationships, child development, social conduct, behaviours and long term well-being for both children and parents. How we parent is as unique as our own fingerprint and draws on lots of factors including:

• How we were parented/modelled parenting

• Personality type

• Levels of our own self-esteem

- Environmental factors, e.g. support, finances, life events, traumatic life events
- Our own well-being and strength
- Emotional baggage

A good tip here is to have a moment to reflect on your parenting. What did your parents do well? What could you do differently for your children? We must be mindful here to not let the parenting pendulum swing too far in the other direction to where we feel it was with us. A happy balance between the two is probably the healthiest place to sit in most circumstances.

Children know that life has rules; they expect sanctions when they have done things wrong and it is normal for our children to hate our reactions sometimes if they are not making the right choices. Remember though, when we are being parents with standards and demands, it is the power we have over our children that they hate at that time, not us. If children make a wrong choice and we remove some screen time, pocket money or social freedom then, over time, our children will learn that they can change the situation to change the outcome. It is this demand on them that activates the process of self-regulation and improved internal motivation towards future choices.

Our sense of self-esteem and belief as parents is tested here, really tested. It must carry us through those times so that we don't alter what we need to do, for fear our children won't like us. Parenting must only go one way and one way only, from us to the child. Otherwise, when our needs are thrown in and we want our children to meet them, things can get very messy!

Children with sadness and low mood need to feel listened to and they need to feel that things are fair. They also need us to have high but realistic expectations of them and their abilities. They need us to nudge them towards positive well-being through love, support, listening, guidance, positive relationships and acceptable boundaries.

The importance of empathy

Now that we know about the physiological, cognitive and emotional differences between what our children experience and what we do, together with the importance of supportive nurture with demands as the the most effective parenting style, we can now glue both of these factors together with an understanding of empathy. Empathy is not easily taught but by modelling it to our children, they can begin to recognise its value and over time, develop and share it with others.

Empathy involves recognising another person's perspective in a situation. It used to be described as putting yourself in another person's shoes. I think it is actually deeper than that. It is more about tapping into your own difficult times and connecting and sharing those feelings to help our children know they are not alone. This is where non-judgmental listening is of the most value, as mentioned in section 2. We are never likely to feel a connection with someone who we feel is judging us, and it may set us back even further not to share our deepest sadness or emotional distress.

Empathy is about stopping to put ourselves in that moment with our child, and to try and connect on that emotional level and understanding. The help comes later when we have truly listened and connected with our child at that level. The earlier we start this the better, but it's never too late. Most problems feel instantly better when we feel someone understands us.

It is only when the empathetic connection has been made, that support can be offered. Without empathy first, trust is compromised and information is more likely to be rejected. This is not about offering optimism or obvious solutions, it is about connecting and finding solutions together. If we can offer this as part of our parenting, our child's sadness and emotional withdrawal will ease over time.

Summary

This book is designed to provide you with the most important emotional and behavioural practice to help you to become an emotions' expert on the psychology of sadness. The more emotionally aware we are, the better support and guidance we can offer to the children and young people in our care.

All children and young people will experience difficult life events that will activate sad feelings. We cannot and should not protect them from such experiences, as we learn from all the rich life experiences that we face. An important part of emotional intelligence and improved well-being is knowing how to deal with difficult emotions, and not to resist or avoid them.

Sadness isn't an enemy, it's one of the many emotions that we need to experience to allow us to feel even happier when times are going well. If our children are sad, it doesn't mean we have failed, it means that they are responsive to life and feeling it wholeheartedly. It means they are alive and can learn to use sadness to understand that most amazing feeling, true awe.

I hope that throughout this book, you have banked many useful strategies as to support the children and young people in your care with greater knowledge and confidence.

Sad - Summary Checklist – little things that can help in a big way!

- Remember that emotional acceptance, not emotional avoidance or resistance, is the key to emotional freedom
- Help your children to learn the importance of being mindful and in the moment. Children who feel sad are usually reliving sad memories and so become suspended

in the past. By developing a mindful approach, we can project ourselves into the present where hopefully, things are better

- Give children choices whenever possible, this makes them feel part of everyday events and less likely to activate sad feelings

- Focus on the positive behaviours from your child, not the negative. By focusing on the things that can be changed for the better, we need to let other things go

- Don't always give children constant direction, as this can make children feel their choices aren't good enough. Allow them to develop their independence and do things for themselves, suggesting possibilities if needed

- Offer high support with realistic but high demands – Authoritative parenting style

- Remember that tough love is important whether they like you or not, as it fosters self-regulation and internal motivations

- Keep relationships strong and positive by connecting emotionally and with empathy

- Try not to transfer adult projections on what children might be feeling, and why they might be doing what they are doing. Remember that their brains are different

- Be human, not perfect. We all make mistakes; we all get things wrong. Make mistakes normal not abnormal

- Recognise your own well-being and needs (BOPS)

- Value and praise the process to success rather than the result. Celebrate effort, determination, hard work and commitment

- Have some set techniques for when things are difficult. Breathing exercises like 3,3,3 (breathe in for 3 seconds, hold for 3 seconds and breathe out slowly for 3 seconds) or 4,7,8 (breathe in for 4 seconds, hold for 7 seconds and breathe out slowly for 8 seconds) really helps children feel calm and cope better; these need to be practised often and not just when things are not going well

- When life is feeling tough, do rest, but don't give up until you reach the result that you want

- Check in with your own well-being regularly and especially when your children's well-being isn't how you want it to be and do your best to reset them through reflective parenting and mindfulness

- Seek support from emotional and behavioural psychologists or your GP if you feel negative self-talk is not improving. CBT approaches can really help

If you and your child have enjoyed The Blinks – Sad (book 4 in this series) then look out for the first, second and third books, The Blinks– Worry, The Blinks - Anger, and The Blinks – Self-esteem, all readily available online and in book stores. Keep an eye out for the fifth book in this series, The Blinks – Shy, due for release late Autumn 2017.

To get in touch on social media, please go to:

Facebook - /Theblinksbooks

Twitter - @BlinksThe

OTHER TITLES IN THE SERIES

The Blinks novels are for younger children from the age of 7. They would benefit when reading the novel with adults as it's never too young to start emotional dialogues – there is no upper age range as no matter your age the core of emotions feels the same.

The Blinks are created from morsels of goodness that all the good folk who have ever lived, leave to the Universe. These could have been left behind by people who you have loved in the past. Their whole purpose is to share their wisdom and kindness with children who need support and guidance in order to promote positive well-being. 'The Blinks – Worry' is the first novel in the Blinks series of books. The first book in the series to help all children and young people understand how worry and anxiety present. It is written as a fiction book with many messages and guidance woven into the stories about Amanda and her friends.

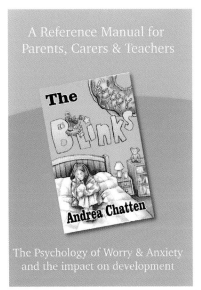

The Blinks books were created to help children, young people and their families understand emotional and behavioural issues. More so, it was to provide strategies and techniques to help manage and change the intensity and duration of problematic behaviours over time. This supportive book provides a deeper understanding of psychology of worrying and how it can impact on other developmental issues including self-esteem and emotions. It also provides lots of 'top tips' of what works best for children and young people whilst growing up, and some activity questions that can be used as a starting point to initiate emotive dialogue or discussion with children.

Robbie's life has never been great, but the events over the last few years have slowly made him more and more unhappy and angry. One day it all gets too much and his anger erupts! A sequence of wrong choices leaves Robbie with a string of problems that need sorting out. Luckily Chika Change-Your-thoughts sees that he needs help at this difficult time. Together with Cale, 'the community bad lad with a heart', Robbie learns just who is responsible for his anger and how to deal with it.

This supportive booklet accompanies the book 'The Blinks – Anger' written specifically for older children and those in their early teens. It provides a deeper understanding of the psychology of anger for parents, carers and teachers, and how anger can impact on other developmental issues and all other emotions. It also provides lots of 'top tips' on what works best for children and young people whilst growing up and some activity questions that can be used as a starting point to initiate emotive dialogue or discussion with children.

In 'The Blinks – Self Esteem' Edition Bladen and Tim are twins who have spent many years being unkind to each other. This has not helped them develop very positive feelings about themselves. This low self-esteem has affected their confidence, friendships, who they believe they are and their happiness. Things have been difficult for many years, but then the unthinkable happens, and Bladen and Tim think that it is their fault. This causes them to dislike themselves even more. Larry Love-Who-You-Are recognises this difficult situation and works hard to help the twins and himself overcome some very personal challenges. This book is for children aged 7+ who want help with learning how to cope with low self-esteem. It is written as a fiction book with lots of messages and guidance woven into the stories about Bladen and Tim and their friends.

This supportive booklet accompanies the novel 'The Blinks – Self-Esteem' written specifically for children and those in their early teens. It provides a deeper understanding of the psychology of low self-esteem for parents, carers and teachers, and how this can impact on other developmental issues and all other emotions. It also provides lots of 'top tips' on what works best for children and young people whilst growing up and some activity questions that can be used as a starting point to initiate emotive dialogue or discussion with children.

Shan is a normal girl in many ways, who has a normal life, but one thing Shan has which many other children don't is buckets and buckets of sadness. Over time Shan has managed to collect many sad memories which replay constantly in her mind and make her feel sad. Things start to get more difficult when one day at school, when given a very important job, Shan makes a seriously wrong choice and is found out by one of her classmates. Shan feels so sad and worried that she becomes ill and hides away in bed, unable to face going to school. Thankfully, Marlowe Mindful sees Shan as someone who is ready for Blinks' support and begins the process of helping her understand her sadness and how to change her feelings for the better.